The Goddess of Gumbo

The Goddess of Gumbo

Poems by Kendra Hamilton

Word Press

Published by Word Press
P.O. Box 541106
Cincinnati, OH 45254-1106

Typeset in Goudy by WordTech Communications LLC, Cincinnati, OH

ISBN: 1933456345
LCCN: 2006930845

Poetry Editor: Kevin Walzer
Business Editor: Lori Jareo

Cover collage: Kendra Hamilton

Visit us on the web at www.word-press.com

To Lorenzo Thomas,
my teacher and mentor,
now bustin' rhymes
with the ancestors

ACKNOWLEDGMENTS

"The Science of Wearing a Dress" has appeared in *Callaloo*. "The Jade Market at Kowloon" was published in *Southern Review*. "At the Frenchman's" was anthologized in *Bum Rush the Page: A Def Poetry Jam*. "Leaving Sedona" and "New Orleans Woman" appeared in *River Styx*. "The Sight" was published in *Callaloo*, along with a version of "Porch Monkey" titled "The Great Depression," which appeared in *Callaloo* and was selected for the journal's 25th anniversary publication, *The Best of Callaloo*. "Where to Find Them" was published in *Shenandoah*. And "Liza, Dawn to Dusk" and "Why I Love Gardenias" were published in *Obsidian III*.

CONTENTS

I. THE BREAK HEART ROAD

THE SCIENCE OF WEARING A DRESS

Something there is in every woman
that wants a grand entrance, craves it.
Far more than chocolate or red moiré silk
worse than a kiss from Montgomery Clift.
She'll stand for hours grappling with perplexity
at Tootsie's two-for-one cocktail dress sale.
All around her bugle beads are snapping off
hangers with a music like computerized pinball
and women, smiling gamely or grimly,
are maneuvering their way about the racks
with a sinuous yet unapplauded grace
like that of pickup ballplayers pirouetting under a hoop.
  At moments like these what's uppermost
in her mind is not the face of the man
who asked her to the ball—but whether to rip
up the phone bill, buy those Ferragamos
half-price at Diamanté's on Main.
Ravishing shoes the color of sea foam
with stiletto heels she just knows
will strike sparks off a stone-flagged step.
  Yes, something there is in every woman
standing rooted in a dress shop
that knows the night will be hers,
that every Japanese lantern on every rooftop
in Dallas will be lit just for her
and that Susan Heyward hip snap she worked
three months to perfect will get a tryout
after all—this night—with "the one."
Though he, not being such a one as can interpret
the arcane cricket whisperings of nylons
in the ladies room, will never know
what it cost her, or how she chose to pay.

The Jade Market at Kowloon

Perhaps it is to avoid some great sadness
that the crowds arrive each day between the hours
of ten and three-thirty, press beneath the Kansu Street flyover
for the Jade Market at Kowloon.

Day after day, the scene is the same,
try though one might to imagine it differently.
A drove of sweating bodies,
old men in black silks and Air Jordans,
dapper men in tailor-made suits,
trim, ivory women, their heavy dark hair
tortured into ringlets or streaked blonde,
and always, always the tourists,
pink acquisitive fingers worshipping the stones,
the ancient loot of warlords and emperors.

There's green jade and white,
brown jade and red, deer carvings for wealth,
tigers for luck, dragons for power,
and no scent stronger than the smell of money.
Not the dai pai dong stalls outside,
nor the mangoes piled high and golden,
a magnet for flies—
as within, the very walls and floor thrum
with a rhythm not felt
since the West sent its spice ships and slave ships
to conquer the world.

For here in Hong Kong,
this marketplace of the world, all we love
and are is on display: from knock-off couture
to the latest high-tech toys,
from twenty-dollar Rolexes hawked on the streets.
to five-carat emeralds and heavy Hawaiian pearls
agleam behind bulletproof glass.

So I know it is an aching hunger
drawing them here, to the Jade Market
at Kowloon, where today
an engineer from Pretoria on leave
from his posting in Beijing eyes
a slim brown girl who'd be colored back home.
Does he dare propose lunch in Ya Ma Tei?

She weighs a chain of amber chips
the color of honey in one tapered hand.
Smooths the polished stones
across her cheeks. Sighs
for a few dollars Hong Kong more.

At The Frenchman's

The woman at the table beside mine is crying.
Painted mouth a round wet O,
back held stiff against all comfort.
I sip Mexican beer cold from the cooler,
rub cubes of ice between my breasts,
smile a distant smile.
I am too hot to be bothered

with anything but the dream on the dance floor:
the thigh-high skirts and cowboy boots,
skin tight jeans, vaquero belts,
the dip and swirl, swing out snap back,
to the chucka-chucka-chucka-chucka rub-board beat.
Voulez-vous dansez, douce cher?

You bet your sweet ass, cowboy.
But it's so hot—
The Frenchman's AC broke down
by the heat from so much flesh,
steam within the stuccoed walls like the heat
rising from the bayou: too thick, laden
with a perfume of things too ripe, too sweet.

Seems like hours since I've danced
and I want to hear you say it, cowboy,
save me from that sad song mad song place,
that *what does it cost me to know you don't want me* place
where you're not waiting and I'm left all alone,
where every word is an unripe persimmon
and the lump in my throat heavier than stone.

But you don't, you won't,
and that woman goes buck wild,
strikes away the hands of her friends,
lurches toward the pool tables,

the fluorescent-lit tableau of tattooed arms
holding someone else—again.

I mark her progress by the snags
in the smooth circling of the dancers,
her shrill counterpoint to Beau Jocque's baritone,
the pool cue held high, the smashed glass,
the laughter... I might laugh, too,

if not for the memory of burning the dolls
you gave me in the sink.
Made so much smoke I scared the dog.
Wild night that was of microdot and mescal down to the worm,
a Lady Schick hammered to its thin blue tongue of steel.
That night I swore if I lived till dawn
I'd never, never again...

But I still love to dance—especially at the Frenchman's.
The thigh high skirts, the cowboy boots
the horses, Harleys and sport trucks out back.
Yes, I love the Frenchman's

despite knowing myself far too well in these women—
Hypocrite danseur in my flat-brimmed hat.
Night after night finds me here, trembling.
This body's not a wart I can just burn
off my soul. So won't you dance with me, cowboy,
just once with me tonight?

THE KHADINE

Now that the dais strewn with rose petals belongs to me,
now that the odalisques chant my name as they carry
honeyed dishes from the Golden Road to the Palace of Sighs,
as their hennaed feet pound the tile floors in time to the song
of the oud and the ney, the whisper of the finger cymbals,
now that they and all this are mine, even my lord's own self
reclining beside me on these embroidered cushions, breathing
the scented air, the wise agree that it was my Beauty
that netted him. "She is like unto the full moon," sing the poets,
and other such nonsense. They compose stanzas to my eyes
in which I figure as Honey-of-Life, Heart's-Ease, Nazgul: the Shy Rose.

But saving only Kislar Aga over there, magnificent in coral silks
and rose gold, he whose ebony hands would have snapped
my neck like the stalk of a lily at a word from his master, my lord—
saving only he, none of those here now know, that it was my Voice
that worked the charm—my Voice and not my eyes or my lips or even
those endless stories of merchants and fishermen, young princes
and princesses, djinni, enchanted gazelles, ships sailing seas of emerald
and blackened brass. My Voice: a sigh, a chant, a whisper deep
as the kemancheh, thready like the ney, rich and full like a santur.
Night after night as cobalt skies frayed to gray, it soared
a descant above the song his savaged pride so long refused to sing.

Beside me now on our scented divan he snores, bored by the poet's verses.
A barbarian to the last—for him the subtleties of the Persian could never
    appeal.
And yet, looking down at him, the slight smile curving his lips as he dreams,
his skin warmed to clear caramel in the candlelight, I feel what I felt and I
    burn.
For one thousand and one nights time was of two days, one bright, one
    desperate,
of two moieties, one safe and one fearful. I'd speak of corpses floating on the
    sea,
precious pearls secreted in its furthest depths. I'd speak of the heavens
where the stars burn without number, none eclipsed save only the brightest,

the sun and the moon. When he'd take me in his arms in his accustomed
    way,
wrapping my hair about his fist, dragging my head back for the kiss—I'd see
the knife in his eyes, not once but every time. I'd close my own to hide the
    bliss.

NEW ORLEANS WOMAN

The Rastafari in Congo Square had marijuana for hair.
"Peace sister" his blessing, and she'd've bought
a button or a tie-dye shirt but for the voice growling
from the wrought-iron fence:
      "Want some lobster, baby?"
The tongue wrapped round the words
like they were dripping herbed butter.
She'd bolted—he'd followed
insistent as men in that city are.
The place, he'd said, was his uncle's,
his intentions he assured her honorable.
      "And you believed that?"
the chorus of girlfriends sputtered.

He had a woman in Arkansas,
she had a husband in Charlotte
so they washed up in the city on a tide
of Jack Daniels Fourth of July weekend.
Later she'd blame Baby Doll
the matchmaking hooker at the dance hall.
Much, much later the no-count husband,
the full moon, even that tired B-movie madam of a city.
But it was her own silver screen sensibility
that betrayed her—the glamour-puss blondes
with swimming pool eyes she imagined stalking
the Quarter, the visions amid the heat and sweat
of taffeta skirts swinging, of men who tasted
of bourbon and brown sugar,
wooed with smooth words
between warm bites of crab.

She couldn't know or want to know saint from sinner
amid so many magnolia-shaded courtyards.
Couldn't resist or want to resist the mingled scents of mimosa
and rain—and when so many were plumbers from Peoria

drinking, dancing, telling Korean grocer gags while their eyes
roamed the shadows seeking some stranger
for the mating dance of moonlight and marsh gas
they'd come for, how could she not want a room
with lace curtains, a man from a riverboat dream?

So, no, cher, the AC didn't work,
what breeze there was barely stirred the curtains
and it was hot, so hot they slipped out at three a.m.
to skinny-dip in a hotel pool no bigger than her kitchen sink.
"New Orleans woman," he called her
and she willed her tattooing heart to calm,
willed sleep though thoughts were pooling
thicker than catfish in cool water.
Oh, to live that legend,
more passionate than history
if dead at twenty-five:
New Orleans woman ...
whose license says El Paso

IN MY MOTHER'S GARDEN, I REMEMBER YOUR TOUCH

I can't see the moon for the clouds
but the night is bright with white blossoms:
peacock orchids, moonflowers, sweet tobacco
silver and pearl in the long blue shadows
and the scent of angel's trumpets
is rising from the damp earth.

The field guide calls them deadly poison,
Jimson weed, datura,
but I love their lush night blooms,
love the kiss of their scent as I
loved your lips against my lips
your teeth against my neck
your strong brown arms
pinning me to grass,
so hot, so hot that night
as if I'd just discovered jazz.

Tonight, drunk on that scent,
the sound of the wind chimes
recalls an eon of longing
in the interlaced echoes that rise
then sink into the arms of the lilies,
the bright-bladed anemones.

I shiver, all infinitives sundered.

Do I hear the sound of your laughter,
smell your scent rising
from the crushed damp grass?

That was long and long ago
and you'll never return.
But I wonder how I'd live without
the breathing summons of that memory,
the hectic kiss of that scent
at the deep blue edge of evening.

LIES TO TELL IN DENVER IN A HEAT WAVE

I ask him, why are there no
French Quarter girls
in Denver?
I hate them anyway with their stick legs

and micro-minis
as I hate bad olive oil pyramided
on shelves
at the Piggly Wiggly

I tell him, one drink
is my limit in the altitude
Afraid I'll fall
and skin my knees

I say, I could fall in love with you
if it weren't so damn hot
but I left
my straw hat
in Atlanta, thinking
I was headed toward cool

And now it's 96 degrees
in the shade
and there the sun is drowning—
Bainbridge, Valdosta

under three feet of water
snakes and
alligators in the trees, fire ants
in the kitchen sink

I say, I could tell you all about the South
all about me
the Spanish moss I call my hair

the way my
mother bleeds Tabasco

when I
sing the blues
the river is the bass line
listen   listen
You can hear the tree frogs crying

IF BEALE STREET COULD TALK

August is a sacred time, a month of holy pilgrimage
in far west Tennessee, so any traveling woman
with a tank full of high test would do well to fight shy
of all things Elvis, roll straight down 40, cross the river,
hang the dogleg over to Beale, find a bar and set.
That's Beale as in Beale Street—home, they say, of the blues.

Now you are a woman who's made it her personal business
to become acquainted with the blues.
You know the place where Handy wrote Memphis into song,
that B.B.'s mama called him Riley. You know
how to dance it—skirt snapping till your skin's
hissing hot and sweat beads pop like spit on an iron.
You know how to moan and groan it
on nights warmed only by Jim Beam and beer,
And because you've been there night after night
after moon-shattered night, you know the spirits
won't come down without a song.
All this you know—but it don't take long to figure
you don't know this place, the tongue this street speaks.

The sun goes down and it's all so bright and yet not tawdry.
Neon blazing but not cheap—retro.
You could get this in Orlando.
They got a House of Blues, a Hard Rock Café
though maybe not a Tater Red's Lucky Mojo and Voodoo Healings.
You think of this town's icons of ill fame: Machine Gun Kelly,
May the Wonder, Temple Drake and her white slaver Popeye.
Could they ever have been born of these power-washed streets?

Place ever gives way to time and the yellow fever dreams
of the lived landscape fade: the tired tap-tap
of the streetwalker's heels at 3 a.m., the Club of Missing Men,
even the blood-soaked balcony at the hotel Lorraine
and whole streets that blazed up like a gas-fed fire after...

The sharp outlines of these tales shimmer, blur
and we hear sound—the pulse of a funky
bass beat from every store-front, the *ka-ching!*
that cash registers sing—but no more stories
in this monument to family pleasure,
this paradise of dimpled tourists' thighs.

Night falls on Beale Street.
Overhead reels a monstrous moon—
earth and flesh both tremble
restless sussurant.
You fumble for your keys.

CANAAN

been so long since i been to Canaan
i ain't been since i fell in love
my man be gone by seven a.m.
too tired, he say, to talk last night
i want to spend just one night less lonely
want to get drunk in love's rose garden

a house, a canopy bed, a garden—
i'll get that when i get to Canaan
like a door prize for falling in love
piling up stuff for a life less lonely
but i know there'll be no talking tonight
and then he'll be gone by seven a.m.

catbirds mewing at seven a.m.
hummingbirds feeding down in the garden
the thought's a cool drink on a hot summer night
not like this endless longing for Canaan
not like the pain of losing this love
or how much i'm scared of that word lonely

mama say you can be alone, not lonely
i don't believe that at seven a.m.
got a shelf full a books that talk about love
but i never drank wine in that sweet smelling garden
never seen the moon rise over Canaan
won't even sleep less he fucks me tonight

why is the talking time never tonight?
why does the waiting time feel so lonely?
been so long since i been to Canaan
that's what i think almost every a.m.
when he's on the road and i'm in the garden
counting pink pills and brooding on love

the books all say no one dies of love

but a voice from the gloom calls out every night
calls dark and restless from the fenceline of the garden
says, step across, i won't let you be lonely
last night i walked there until seven a.m.
and knew in my heart i'd never see Canaan

so i'll drink to Canaan, to falling in love
to the pink pill a.m, but don't come home tonight
let me be lonely—let me burn down that garden
just let me be lonely—and burn down that garden

LEAVING SEDONA

Sign on AZ Rte. 89:"Fire Danger Is Moderate Today"

  Thirty miles past Sedona on the Oak Creek Canyon trail
seems light years into this paleozoic womb.
I strain to see the tree-crowned lava caps,
the road twisting-coiling like a ribbon of floss
between the teeth of the red rock bluffs and the creek.
After LA's endless sunshine, after stick-dry Phoenix
with its sudden, shocking storms of flame, this blush
of cool, of wet against my pores is a great beatitude
and my heart is light.
     They call this forest Coconino, and here
my botanical pride is greatly humbled. I see piñon,
well, short pines and tall, and spruce and birch
with peeling bark, but this is not my place.
This land has secrets I'd not plumb had I
all the summers I've lived plus all those left to me.

At the Ranger Station and Scenic Overlook

  Indians. I've been traveling the West six weeks,
crossing reservation lands—Yavapai, Hualapai, Pima
—seeing little but mesquite and mobile homes.
Here at last, I've found them. Indians. And I, who know
too well what it is to be stared at, I'm afraid to look.
They are selling crafts beside a Park Service
book kiosk—lovely soapstone bears, beadwork,
turquoise, arrowheads. I'm mortified. I have
too little cash to buy, too little nerve to ask a question.
  Then, too, there are the faces—far darker than my own
and craggy, alien. They are Hopi. Dressed as Hopi.
In Arizona Diamondbacks T-shirts and jeans.
The deep-set eyes in those deep-brown faces look
at me, I think, with accusation. *We know your kind,*
they seem to say, *though we know not what you do here.*
Tossing their lampblack hair. *Cliff cities in these hills*

knew our kind eleven thousand years before yours
were dragged here, filthy, in chains. I think of Buffalo Soldiers.
Burn with shame. I snap a quick shot of the canyon,
slate clouds lowering over the red-breasted hills.
Using plastic at the bookstore, I buy a field guide.
Hop in my car and fly.

At the Powwow Inn, Rte. 66, Tucumcari, New Mexico

  There's a Kachina doll painted on the motel door.
A blanket framed on the desert pink walls.
  This is the last straw.
  Storms have hounded me from Apache lands to Navajo.
Drops the size of bullets pelting the car, great lances of lightning
scissoring the inky sky. And everywhere the signs: KACHINA DOLLS!
PETRIFIED WOOD! AUTHENTIC INDIAN CRAFTS! Taiwan made.
What is this poisonous nostalgia ribboned through our culture?
We mourn what we've destroyed, and seek not to make amends, but
resurrect it through cheap trinkets. Kachina dolls, lawn jockeys,
dream catchers, mammy cookie jars side by side on the shelves.
  In the gift shop at the Powwow Inn, there's a life-sized Indian doll.
He has two braids, a turquoise headband topped with a turkey feather,
a magnificent necklace of bone over his chambray shirt.
I imagine he's also for sale.
  "Tucumcari" is an Apache word that means "lookout."
I snap the mannequin's picture. I am keeping
a sharp look out.

ARIADNE AUF NAXOS, ALABAMA

I. On Seeing Dionysus at the Hydraulic Road K-mart

Iakhos, holy one, lightly treads linoleum aisles past
lawn mowers, half-price books, Martha's pastel towels.
A cart, leopard-drawn, draped in grapevine, trundles
at his heels. Square-hipped shop girls sigh and sweat.

They hear the maenads singing—though there are those
who see only someone's dad, taller than many, better looking
than most—a deacon in somebody's church? Proof,
I say, our world's not odd enough for outlandish you.

Or contrarily that, of this parking lot world smelling so
strongly of diesel fumes, you are the savior. Marooned here
among the adenoidal girl singers and jumbo tubs of peanut
butter, I could be your Ariadne, lost and longing to be found.

It is spring, your feast-time. Leaves are on the vines. We broach
new wine to pour libations, and we grow young…we grow young.

II. The Triple Goddess Learns the Electric Slide

We broach new wine to pour libations. We grow young,
each year younger. Yes, the crown grays, breasts sink
lower on our bellies. Still we don our dancing shoes,
our flashing rings, set bits of crystal clashing in our ears.

Still we curl our lashes, straighten our hair so as, aswirl
in scent, in silks, to dance again our spiral dance, stepping
forward, swaying back, all those rows of toes tip-tapping
an electric slide, in perfect time, into timelessness.

So, yes, it's just the Elks Lodge, as you say, just a group
no longer young in heels, a silly line dance, four-four beat.
Yet each is more: crone who in her prime grows young,

skin fresh, elastic, on her tongue no foretaste of the lees

at the bottom of the cup. Spirit, birdlike, darts amongst us:
we wax, we wane, stars rise, the earth exhales a dark perfume.

III. *Ariadne auf Naxos, Alabama*

I wax. I wane. The earth exhales her dark perfume
on this night blacker than emigration, than the darkest
night of separation, when even the stars above are red
and sullen. A thing I know. We're falling out of love.

It's said the sweets of life are for the mad. Well, I've
been that for you. Left my home blood-hot, candent
for the flush of skin on skin. Now I subsist on glimpses,
your distant voice acrackle on a mobile phone.

You found the thread hid deep within the labyrinth
of me, followed without effort. Your kiss my resurrection,
I came blinking from that world below. A thing I know—
for me there's no return to the numbness of before...

So I think now, never was death so alive as on that day
you came, breathing miracles which now you murder.

IV. *Ariadne's Plaint Continues*

You came, breathing miracles which now you murder
not respecting even spring—the finches chip-chip-
chipping at the feeder, tulips carving dabs of blood
on the picket fence, freedom not a hate or a forgetting

not yet at least. And still I cannot rest, have bad dreams:
a woman came with hands and eyes like mine, hair like night
perfumed with musk, and she'd been weeping, weeping.
I know her thready whisper *how I died* as my heart

greyly failed within me. And still you call and still I come,

as if forever's now were where we stood, were still
to give. I've accepted what you can't—there's no appeal
from reason. So soon and very soon I'll have to save myself,
leave this house to mourn its builder, find another,
breathe the no that fate won't let me yes. This time.

V. *Theseus Recalls His Days Under Sail*

Breathe the no that fear won't let her yes? This time
she may. What holds her here I know—thirty years of history:
tiny hands on faces in a playpen, or dumped into a common bath.
Her smell, the very texture of her skin, like innocence itself.

Dark of heart, they'd say who knew us well, for me to claim
her love, her trust, all the luminous whole of singing her—
for cease from exploration, I cannot; shake off
my commitments, I will not, not even for the secret sweet

of her. It's at the heart of who I am. I love the calls at 3 a.m.
Montreal? I'm there. I leave a house that sleeps to board
a jet bound who knows where. Just like the haze gray
days of setting out, sailing where the skies and sea are blue

and the women slim, hot, next to nothing on. Still I hold.
Our brief days grow briefest, she says. I don't let go.

VI. *Dionysus Speaks in Dreams and Portents*

Their brief days already briefest, I just eased
the letting go. For heart-starved, sucked frail by spring's
unregenerate bright sun she began to pine, to fail.
In his greediest paws I saw her going down, down,

down to dolor while his pride peacocked fat, well-fed
on her red currant pout. This my mystery profaned
for I am the merging/the madness both gentle
and terrible... which she does not flee. One whisper

from me leaves him sleepless, cigarette in hand, while
in a room across the river she sprawls in sweet
apostasy, grapevine twined about her bed. The skirl
of flutes, scent of wine arising, her heart opens

like hibiscus to my words. *The thread is not lost:*
if I be your labyrinth, you'll find it in the dark.

VII. *Shopping for the Sacred Marriage*

She would find them in the dark, but the labyrinth
is garish with fluorescent light, the six hundred
thread count sheets she seeks sold out—nor do the cheap
chenilles, crochets offered in their stead have power to tempt.

She trips away. No more the nibbling sharp-toothed hours.
And that last thread of his voice raveling from the raw edge
of this current ease? She snips it, ruthlessly, away.
The absolute stars are still overhead, spring breeding

glory of the snow and crocus below, and she knows
the one note to resolve her discordant passions
into perfect silken tune won't sound. Love him or end
it, neither stops the rhythm of the dance, the skirl

of flutes, the fragrant scent of libation. Even here, in this place,
Iakhos treads the cold white aisles, palm outstretched for her.

II. THE SPANISH MOSS I CALL MY HAIR

UNDONE

You've cut the greens from your own ground

washed them in clear water

handed each leaf up to the light from a north-facing window

You've torn the greens

tossed them in olive oil garlic pepper

Dished them up hot

Hunger sharpens the savor

You are alone and angry

Chewing hard   teeth closing with an audible click

tongue pressed against palate to bruise the last bitter metal mustard heat

of the pot likker down your throat

Then

less a taste than a sound

less a crunch than the collective suck of your womenfolks' teeth:

grit in the mustards

The voices a sigh:

Didn't clean them greens like a good woman should

THE SIGHT

She is five and if she crouches
between the dropped leaves
of the mahogany tabletop
no one can see her.
  Their voices rise and fall
and break in waves
against the swirled grain,
red brown and smelling
like the bottle of lemon oil
mama keeps in the hall closet.
Soft or pointed like a whittled stick
the voices whiffle the crocheted doilies,
ping against the brass candlesticks,
rattle the dishes in the china cabinet.
  Sometimes she hears secrets this way.
Once she looked Miz Boatwright
dead in the eye and told her
she was due in June and
the baby would be a Cancer.
Her eyes they say were spooky
when she said it. She knows
too much they say.
Their eyes follow her now
when she's not looking,
when she's mixing cakes
and baking them in her E-Z Bake Oven
or dressing her dolls for school.
  The table has iron feet with
claws and leaves that look
like wings. If it were
a storybook table she thinks
the feet would grab her
and they'd fly east of the sun,
west of the moon.
  Sometimes now the voices
talk about her about her sight,

how it's just like Aint Geneva's.
Geneva wore glasses, cat-eyed
with pearlie rims—even when they
put her in the ground last year.
She doesn't want to wear glasses.
She doesn't want the kids
to call her four eyes.

ON EASTER STREET

on Easter Street, the woman has a blue tattoo
of bruises on her arm and the silence at breakfast
is thicker than day-old oatmeal.

he's a Navy man,
eyes like an autopsy waiting
to happen—a man alone,
but for the woman,
the five daughters.
and they fret him.

he doesn't want their soft hands.
he wants to bring the brawling ports
home. he doesn't want her family eyeing
his raggedy Buick. he wants salt air
and monotony, days that swell and billow,
billow and bottom out, each one like the one
before. he doesn't want the house
on Easter Street. he wants men smoking
Kools, women with an hourly rate.
he doesn't care who has to pay.

THE GOOD FUNERAL

after Stevie Smith

No one heard the dead man
      They were all too busy singing
And the son shouting "*daddy! daddy!*"—
      launching himself at the coffin
It took three men to wrestle him back
      so no one heard the dead man
the moans so softly lingering
      as if he were drowning but not yet gone—
that was I think why I heard him

Everyone loves a good funeral
      a hand-clapping palm-waving funeral
a deep-singing hard-crying funeral
      You leave full of fire and fried chicken
eyes red head throbbing happy somehow
      The dead man loved his good times too
Never to return

He was swimming and then he was drowning
      and the woman beside him had long been beside him
though not his wife they said
      A chill in his heart surprised him
cold creeping up from his toes to his chest
      And his wife at home they said

The widow is stolid still
      face like a plate wiped clean of care—
and Piedmont earth six rectangular feet
      excavated from her chest
She is silent amid the singing

She looks cold her hands look cold
For it's never been warm enough never
So the dead are always saying—
though no one can hear for the singing

WHY I LOVE GARDENIAS

Bruised gardenia petals line the rain-wet path
past the sagging gray slats of the smokehouse.
Weeds thigh-high and bowed with a shimmering weight
of wet trail dark moist caresses on my new denim stride.
Mornings in spring the smell of gardenia and pine
is like coffee in the kitchen—urgent, demanding
like a kiss from a woman not your sister.
This steamy day the rain-lashed petals creamy
at the centers stained warm tea-leaf brown at the tips
give off a Jurassic effluvia of mold and molt.

Many days I've walked the straw fields dizzy
with sunlight, leaped the red banks of the branch
and raced to the house on the hill where waiting
I knew were the old man's best: Sara Lee pound cake
wrapped tight against ants, strong coffee thick and sweet
with blackstrap molasses, and pressed into my palm
as I left, one gardenia from the bush beneath his window.
I never saw the clutter, the dust and dog hair,
the bits of chewed paper and bone blooming in the corners
and under the sink. Only his eyes, blear and yellow
like beer turned flat in the sun but warm like the sun,
and his hands, brown and worn as an old saddle, cradling
the frail bone cups his mother's kin had drunk from.

I stand where I stood before. What can I do but remember?
His name is on my lips, in the breeze that stirs the straw field,
in the morning chatter of the jays: a cryptic shout, a prayer
in the secret gardenia hearts.

PORCH MONKEY

She has no desire. She has a ring,
a ring on her hand that she twists
and twists again. She has a word,
one word in her chest that pushes
its way on an ache of air to her tongue.
But she does not speak it, will not
say its name. Here where she sits
she cannot see the corn spreading its arms

twisting its way up the rope
of the sun or the cotton's brazen
white blooms. She cannot see the men
in the field or the stone from the field
they were clearing. So many stones:
egg white, flinty grey, pink-flecked,
sun-warmed, black with blood.
There were three shotgun blasts from the field

that day. For the women at the well
it was a signal they knew, like a rattler's
hiss from the deeps of the hawthorne
thicket, and they hurried away. She stood
dreaming at the hand crank, listening
to the bucket suspended below,
the creak of hemp, the plash of thick water
clover honey brown, and the flies

bottle blue and thick as her thumb,
buzzing loud as mowers. Later
they told her what happened to Sweet,
his fall from the wagon, the stone arching
to meet him, how no one moved, then all
moved at once. They told her this those
hard men, faces and hands of tree
bark, tears standing in their leaf brown eyes.

Now it is she who does not move.
She's ill, they tell her. They do not
make her work, slap her hands
from the biscuit dough, say she'll curdle
the milk in the churn. She spends her
afternoons on the porch where the wind
in the pines seems a live thing bent
on thrashing all the mockingbirds and

whippoorwills from their nests.
They complain so loudly the voice
of the child at her knee disappears—
disappears into the radio's buzz, the low
songs of women, disappears
into the scraping of cicadas,
the hot, hot tongue of longing—
the sun.

FALSE RIVER[1]

The river is a woman in a long grey dress,
     You and I turn in her arms.

In the city, we make
          calculations, cogitations, watch
                    the news, pay our bills, make
scratches in red across
          reams of white paper.
                    Oh, city of deadlines, city of
smokestacks pouring unseen grit
          on the heavy air, city of
                    traffic stalled on the
Eye-Ten-Eye-Twelve-Split,
          we pray to your gods forty
                    hours a week, with fifteen-minute breaks
every four, and smile—
          for beyond the city,
                    the river waits.

The river is a woman in a long, grey dress,
     Sun mango-ripe twixt her arms.

On the drive, you feel her presence,
          her green darkness invading
                    the car. You can almost smell her,
as you take in the sights: jeweled berries
          winking in flats from the side
                    of the road; a crumbling
grit-stained bridge, arching
          gull grey into the breeze's
                    invisible tarbrush; signs

---

[1] The False River is an oxbow of the Mississippi that flows through New
Roads, Louisiana, which is the birthplace of Ernest Gaines and the center of
his fictional universe.

for "Marksville," "Rougeon,"
        "Bayonne." You've not gone
                far enough, your cares still shove
pebble hard against your eyelids.
        You must go farther, farther
            to the river.

The river is a woman in a long, grey dress,
        Clouds aflame, air heavy and warm.

Men have been here before you.
        Men with slave blood
                and stained hands
been here before you,
        strung this life, this land
                in words like crickets
singing on a fishing line,
        like strawberries burning
                on the green-dark air:
They've told of mulattoes,
        cotton-mouthed hate twisting their guts;
                sheriffs in ten-gallon hats; Cajuns swearing
murder, riding red-handed;
        and the dark people, eyes closed,
                hidden deep in the cane.
A ribbon flashes quicksilver between the trees.
        You've seen her at last. The river.

The river is a woman in a long grey dress.
        Wears the moon like a shiny love charm.

Men here pay you tribute—
        bearing bream, green and shining with the oil
                their formation, they want to make you
the queen of the river.
        The flesh they grill for you
                is white and tender.
Their blue eyes are pearl-bright
        in the moonlight. Beer,

they bring you,
cold from the cooler,
crawfish, sweet and hot —
scorch your tongue.
Moonrise finds you sailing the river
on a mahogany bed
four feet off the ground.
Invite me, invite me in,
say the man's eyes, pearl-bright
in the moonlight.
You've been here before, child of sorrow,
you and the master's son—no, just
dreamed of this bed,
draped in nets like
a robe whose hem is plucked
by whining night children
begging a drink of water.
Invite me, invite me in,
say the eyes, pearl-bright
in the moonlight.
The river's five hundred feet deep,
that's what he'd said when you asked.
It was noon and you'd been swimming,
tangling your feet in the river's cool skirts,
and at his words
a cavern filled with fish
and many-fingered lake fronds
opened up beneath
you, opens up now
beneath your legs tangled in cool white sheets:
Invite me, invite me in,
say the man's eyes.

Shall you close yours,
pretend to sleep?
Dream of the river ?

The river is a woman in a long grey dress.
Come let us turn in her arms.

51

The river is a woman in a long grey dress.
Oh, how we burn in her arms.

WHERE TO FIND THEM

Wear boots, he tells me, cause even in November
the sun can draw that old copperhead from his hole
to the nearest warm rock. Nothing to warn you,
not a rattle or a hiss. *Wear boots, thick ones.* So I do.

We make our way, Uncle Junior and me,
through a ditch thick with bramble across a hayfield,
the stalks waist high and blinding bright
in the bleak autumn sun. *Are you sure this is the way?*
I get that look.

Junior can't stop talking to me about us—the Hills—
owners of these red-shouldered hills
My stamp on you, all of you, he swaggers.
I hear only snatches—I'm all out of breath.

Just look at your brother, he goes on.
Don't wanna see no slouching boy, I told him.
Sit up in church like a king!
Acts like he owns that church now
I know this next bit by heart—
Well, we built it brick by brick after slavery.

The graveyard, when we get there,
is as he has said:
tumbledown, full of weeds.
An obelisk guards
the white man's sleep
while the graves of the enslaved
are sunk below the level of soil.
That's how we know they are there.
There are no recent graves
and, of the house, only the foundation stone remains.

The pines sway and sigh overhead

lost in their dreams of the eyes of starlings.
A bobwhite sounds his double note
A few oak leaves rattle
against the lichen-covered stone
with a dry papery scraping
like that of eggshells
in the sink.

I peer into the well where thought sighs
deeper than loneliness.
I speak their names.

LIZA, DAWN TO DUSK

Liza was her name,
a name buried deeper than Jeff Davis's gold.
Never spoken
but not forgotten.

Dusk was when they thought of her,
   when the mules and oxen
     that had owned their skins slunk back
to Jim Hill's tin-roofed sheds
   and those young men—smelling the blood
     of hay on their hands, smelling the greens
and ham from the kitchen,
   hearing the voices of bobolinks
     and women singing slow blues
amid the clangor of cast-iron pots—
   recalled who they were,
     sons of Jim Hill,
sucked the last bitter metal
   of tobacco juice from the plugs
     cut at noon, spit once
and went indoors.

Dusk,
the time of full bellies
and bone-weariness,
time enough for Liza.

Alice, it was known in that wordless way
of the country-bred, had a look of her,
swung her hips about the kitchen
dishing up greens and cornbread
for all the world like Liza,
though not so tall as Liza
and not so dark . . .

Liza in the kitchen, skin like sorghum

standing in a glass jar in the sun,
        Liza at her milking, muscles clenching
then rippling smooth as her fingers
      stroked the tensile teats
for the hiss, the thin, blue gruel.
        Liza, a long countrywoman's stride
down the rusty rows of corn,
      ladeling water into tin cups
        for the men, dirt-streaked, sweating,
stinking . . .

Her biscuits, men said,
would make you slap your mama.
Don't look too hard, they whispered.
Jim Hill hadn't the sense of a hog in hay
where that one was concerned.
Cut Hamp Speakes nigh to death.
Nothing but trash, but still a white man.
And for the nigger, Big Boy, the lash and the bit.
Good boy, too, worth every bit two thousand . . .

The telling
a thing of moonshine and mare's-nests
by tellers born to lie.

They said:

When Liza went to live in the white man's house,
they dared not tell his mam. She died blind
as a broomstick to what all the county knew.
Forty slaves, the white man had, forty slaves
and Liza in his house.

     "A sin," the biddies clucked,
         "a sin and a shame the way that ..."
—Christian ladies dare not speak the name
        —"...sashays around..."

Then came the children, the girl, the two boys.
The town talked itself to a swelling bubble:
Jim Hill needn't think they'd swallow it—no, not long.
"Such a fine daddy—and his mama!"
How they'd pinwheel in their graves
to know what the county knew.

    Voices rising:
        "They'd've sold the heifer South!"
    Oh, yes. Had they known.

Then,
midday's edges bright and sharp
as crystal bits in a creek bed,
Liza'd wheel the buggy
into town, strike dumb every
laughing, lying tongue
on the deacon's porch.

They said:

When candlelight Liza took down her hair,
it was thick and Cherokee black,
blacker than the branch's downstream flow
on a full moon night.

They see:

Jim Hill watching,
watching, in the day
with an angry raptor's gaze
at night they doubt
he's much tamed . . .
stretching one sunburnt hand
toward the fluttering wick.

They know:

Despite the town and all its talk,

despite his sisters' prayers,
he'll never marry.
Not with the red nigger moon glaring
a halo about his head's fox-thatch,
not with the horizon
just another long loop
of Liza's
lampblack
hair.

SOUTHERN LIVING

I am cut and bruised, my nails broken.
I have found love and my lover is ungentle.
There's a many-hued bruise beside my left knee,
three on my right leg at the ankle and the thigh,
a new-formed scar on my left shin where she cut
me—she didn't mean to. But I fear
I grow obsessed, neglect my looks—my hair
grows wild. This is what it is to love in middle life
and I praise God that She has blessed me
with a love like this before I die.

I lavish this passion on my house and garden
I have never felt this for any man. To walk
through my own picket fence, to climb
my steps, survey what I have done...
the painted ferns and adder's tongue dappling
the shade bed, the azaleas and lilacs
resurrected from the dead, each bed dug
and planted myself, the quartz-hard clods
broken with these two hands, on my knees,
pouring sweat like a baptism—
here I've come to know rapture at last.

The house I had before was small and dark
and I loved a dim, cramped love while I lived there.
The man who shared that space loved nothing
that I loved though in his way he was devoted.
On this barren ground I made my first garden
and watched it fail unsprouted seed by withered stem
by blighted stalk. I fought that soil as I fought
the stony clay of his heart, yet in the end
every precious glimpse of green
went dead brown from the roots.

Let us say the names together:
heart-leaf, barrenwort, rose campion, fairies thimbles.

Feel the meditative music of the names:
Goat's rue, lady-by-the-gate, queen-of-the-meadow.

To love a garden is to be in love with words:
with potageries and racemes, corymbs, hispids, and corms.
To love a garden is to be in love with possibility
for it can never, almost by definition, ever be complete:
To love a garden is to be in love with contradiction:
ravished by order yet ever open to the wild.
But more than all these, to love a garden is to find
your one true lover, for a garden can't survive its maker,
will die with the one who loved it, with only a sudden
spray of roses in June amid a derelict tangle of wood sorrel
and sumac to tell an eye that can read the land
that either of you was ever there.

DEEP COUNTRY

They stare at me from the living room wall:
Mama sunburnt, smile reckless,
braid tossed by the wind,
Daddy a notch of worry between
his thick brows, elbow linked with hers.
He is a city boy trying not to sneeze
and this is deep country.

They are so young—painfully,
coltishly, awkwardly young,
fresh from one year's teaching
in the York County schools,
one year's courting among all
the other young brown teachers.
They are long-legged and skinny
yet burning with the newness of those tired,
peeling, separate-but-equal schools.
And handsome.

Mama so fine
the boys had clamored round for years
yet so shy she stood up
her own prom date.
Daddy with a horn player's dash and
somewhere out of the frame
a red Catalina with white trim and fins.
A dragster, a pool shark—tamed by the war.
Now a military precision, an exactitude
of bearing. Did it scare her
this arrogance, this grace?
Was it a thrill?

They have what is needed:
their parents' consent
and a chicken wire bower to be

painted white and decked
with summer flowers.
Of all that awaits them, it's not
their place to know.

Deep in the country two weeks till
they wed, her tea-length fall
of lace is ready, the preacher
is coming from Rock Hill Baptist Church,
and Aunt Geneva's rose bush is heavy with blossoms.
They are sure—she is smiling.

He'll move forward in a white dinner jacket
to bring back sorrow.

HIGH FIDELITY

Those autumn Fridays after the stadium kliegs dimmed,
the last paper cups and hot dog wrappers speared from beneath
the bleachers, the last football pads locked away, the last tail lights
of the last car winked from the parking lot, then the party would
    begin.
A man in braces and black flannels, a woman's thick dark hair
ribbon-caught, a stack of shiny vinyl beside the hi-fi.
They'd sing: *You better come on in my kitchen—it's raining outdoors.*

Midnight saw a spill of young teachers dancing, drinking, front porch
to kitchen table. Sofas pushed back to frame the butterfly swing
of jewel bright skirts, bid whist and Lucky Strikes in the kitchen,
disjointed talk of the game, the drum major's new step, Principal
    Green
and his high water pants, and that pretty new teacher in English B.
Host and hostess basting together the threads of gossip, wit,
idle mendaciousness into a crazy quilt of story, of song.
Yes, *come on in my kitchen—it's raining outdoors.*

Then the record skipped: stiletto heel scuffs on the good wood floors,
the scent of stale tobacco, water rings on the mahogany veneer,
and it was five, ten, then thirty years with no high fidelity blare,
no buddies drunk on the moon's benison and daddy's dark rum
    punch.
All alone at last, unseeingly together, listening to the wind
rustling the pines, the sound of winter coming dry long so.
No one in the kitchen when it's raining outdoors.

THE MEMORY OF WATER

Charleston, S.C., June 2004

The image on the slide looks just like Holland
Blond marsh, wheeling gulls, a brassy sky above
Widen the picture frame enough, all the pieces fit
Even the wanderer I've become may find a place.

Blonde marsh, wheeling gulls, the sky brazen overhead
And a house with a grape arbor I can't seem to find.
The wanderer I've become not yet at the place
Of repose—not final, of course, just a sense of home.

It's the time of green grapes at the house that I can't find.
I wonder if the porch swing is still there?
She's gone to her repose while I'm still seeking home.
Only the smell of marsh lingers—you could never mistake it.

I wonder why the porch swing would still be there
When nothing else I knew has remained the same?
Oh, the smell of marsh, of course—no one could mistake it,
An acrid, fetid reek? I say the smell of life.

But clearly, nothing else has remained the same.
A smooth expanse of asphalt swallowing the wild.
And we roar past, windows sealed against the reek—life
Is so much more than being stuck in traffic.

A smooth expanse of asphalt has swallowed the wild,
Though beneath are streams, miles of pipe, some of it collapsed.
Stuck in traffic no one hears the soft suck and sputter
Of water, the creaking gulls as they bob on the waves.

The city slowly calcifies over streams, miles of pipes.
The city builds new bridges over the water.

Is this a story that has an end or just keeps repeating?
Widen the picture frame enough, all the pieces fit.

And from a great distance, it all looks just like Holland.

URBAN RENEWAL

As if concentrated from morning mist they appear:
brick and stone, frame or stucco, secret piazzas
cloaked in jasmine or ivy.

This is the landscape of my earliest days,
live oaks straining through slabs of cracked pavement,
a pitiless sun overhead, the smell of the sea.

Over these rutted streets, I once picked my way
to Condon's for my once-yearly Buster Browns,
to the corner store for comic books or giant dills—

only a quarter!—to the Battery arm in arm with first love.
Strangled on the hates held long and long
to the city's withered gray heart I fled

many years past only to return at last
drawn by a hunger I neither understand nor
bother to name. And here, now, in the rapture

between dawn and full day, the city lies revealed
strangely void, from the Crosstown to the sea,
strangely empty of the life that once stirred its streets.

Where are the children? I don't see them walking
to school or laughing and wet from the river, or even
annoying all and sundry as they dart between cars.

The very schools stand as if gutted.
And in the once-forbidden zone south of Broad
no lights bloom—the only movement is that

of the elders striding slowly, almost without sound
through the morning damps, and the clattering
trucks and ladders of workmen, passing among homes

magnificently maintained where no one appears to live.
This, I'm told, is the fate of many a lovely aged city,
in Majorca or Portugal, wherever there's sun and sea

and the past stretches languidly back like a lovely
long-necked woman just roused from sleep.
In the city of my birth bitter oleander blooms in masses

at the point where the rivers meet the sea. Pelicans
and gulls wheel and dive in their accustomed dance.
And the day-star sinks to its ocean bed to rise another day.

Pine Wood Elegy

Stiffer today I remember more limber mornings
when we'd don the loincloths of Tarzan and Jane,
walk side by side to our live oak oasis
to face the armies of the Monkey King.
A creek that cut through flowing south to the river
and the triple-noted call of the white-throated sparrow
our private sign as we stalked one another
around brambles, over gullies, through thickets
of myrtle, tangles of smilax, supple jack, pine.

I used to be all angles, knock-kneed, and you all rounded curves.
I used to catch snakes with my bare hands, hornets in glass jars.
I used to pad barefoot on that carpet of pine needles, Yemassee
    silent.
You never wanted me to come—I was just a girl.

It's fall now and the light is fading and there are
no easy answers to the questions that linger.
You've grown tall and straight, my angles have
softened. You even take my hand to steady
my hop across the drought-dwindled stream.
We're filled with longing though nearer now
than we've been in years. The carpet of needles
is ruddy, thick, soft beneath our feet.

Do you remember the painted faces at Halloween, the moccasins
    from GEX?
Do you remember hide-and-seek in the canebrake, the air shattering
    with birdsong?
Do you remember the lilac haze of the wild bay in bloom, the
    garlands I'd weave of jessamine?
You were always talking, you smile. You never would shut up.

I'm silent when we find them, though, the graves
amid the moss-hung pines—of Hattie and Moses and

the baby James, the other names erased by time.
Never knowing who they were, every journey ended here,
so we move lightly between the stones, wary of a step
that might disturb their rest, though only yards beyond
is the chain link fence to the Buick dealership
and the main road into town. One by one its lights blaze
through the dusk. A cold blue voice sounds over the intercom.
With the last guttering candle flame of sunset we turn
to go—and promptly lose our way.

I imagine the forest misses us, wants to hold us fast.
I imagine she'll give us back the smoke, the angels, the moonless
    nights of deep haze and no stars.
Then cold, afraid, I imagine the struggle is for nothing—we'll die
    before we live.
Something fulfilled this hour. Something lost, foretold.

ODE TO BILLY ECKSTINE

Fifteen hours by car, bougainvillea to white pine,
fifteen hours of trying not to watch the blacktop
seal the bleeding gash of the red hills,
not watching the trees, leafless here and black
from three straight days of rain, fifteen hours
by car to Uncle Melnutt's funeral, fifteen minutes to go
when we spot it. Not civilization—but an oasis:
Junebug Moss's store, forsythias flaming on the walk
an early dogwood spitting singed blossoms, rusted topiary
frames and a thirty-seven Chevy up on blocks.
Too early for boiled peanuts—but maybe some vinegar chips?
A spray of gravel, a car door groans and I'm on my way
before the sputtered protest can be heard.
"Just stretch your legs, city boy," I tease.
"Ain't no Klan around here."

I'm lying of course
          what with the steel
guitars inside
          Junebug's wet tobacco eyes
across the chewed
          wood counter
of childhood
          Hand gripping mama's
Mister Junebug
          you'd call him then
You doubt he'd
          know you now
So "Salem Lights "
          you say
"One-eighty-six "
          his reply A jingle
of coins
          then the old man's sigh
"You heard the news?"

News?
You trace the grillwork
        about his eyes
News?
        "Billy Eckstine's dead "

Spin of a vinyl disc and *"Ohhhhh Billy!"*
Mama's heels are doing a mambo across her waxed wood floor—
"Ohhhh Billy!"—Mama'n Aint Vera in big straw hats, spread skirts
a sepia-tinted Easter parade on the hood of Melnutt's Ford.
Later that night there'd be dancing, sweating, hand slapping,
full throats belting the songs on the phonograph, and that man's
voice so like a velvet dress and chocolates a girl would flat crave
a country boy's kiss. *"Ohhhhh Billy!"*— Vera's tale the best
Her first trip North, Melnutt's railroad buddies sneaking her
backstage at the Savoy—Ella, Sarah taking their turns,
Duke at the baton, then Billy stepping up to the mike.
Her eyes grow gardenia blossoms at every telling:
"It was years before I knew what I'd seen that nigh.t "

Ohhhh Billy!
        Your light
on every country
        counter fading
in just three words
        from tobacco-stained lips
And just when did
        they take you off
that jukebox?
        In the still of
the night I'm listening
        for your bitter
chocolate voice
        to save me
and it's
        silent
forever
        still

Let us slay black bears, torch whole screaming cities
of sweet olive and pine, let's face the music and dance.
And Junebug takes the mike: *"Nineteen fifty-one "* his rasp,
"on leave with the boys," flash of a gap-tooth grin.
"Freezing our cans off in Korea, then two weeks
stateside. Never forget it: Trey Charley Matthu
Clem and me turned loose in Californy.
That's when we saw him. That man's voice
was smoother than turkey bourbon on ice."
His shadow burns my lips too dry to smile.
I turn to go. *"Don't forget your change,"*
he says, tobacco eyes smoking.

So we head out
        thin sun
a knife blade
        on oyster gray
clouds
        City boy
knows all the words
        so "Say It Isn't So "
"Blue Moon "
        "Bewitched"
ring out over
        the roe-red hills
I sing too
        anemones
sea stars
        coral polyps
in all the colors
        of the deep
blooming in my eyes

RICE

You speak of the rivers of your homeplace far to the north.
How you'd leave the city in summer for the long trek
to Minnesota, then gather at the creekside in boats,
singing, to beat the grasses till they yielded their sweet black grains.

Here beside the Edisto, rice is a bitter memory:
a darkened barn, a bright brass anklet, a chain,
a people once wild hearing the songs of a people
once free, sick for the rivers of home.

Brass ankle—I thought it simply meant light skin.
But in this ornery riverbank town it's a deadly insult,
you say, from days of white heat, green rivers, long past.

I'm boiling the water for a pot of rice, sifting white
translucent grains in water, an act so familiar now made strange
by the spell of your voice, the warble of your courting flute.

Kendra Hamilton is an award-winning writer living in Charlottesville, Virginia. She holds an M.F.A. from Louisiana State University. Her personal essays have appeared in *BrightLeaf: New Writing of the South and Southern Cultures;* her poetry has been published in *Callaloo, Shenandoah, The Southern Review, River Styx, Obsidian III,* and the anthologies *Bum Rush the Page: A Def Poetry Jam, The Best of Callaloo,* and the forthcoming *The Ringing Ear,* an anthology of Afro-Southern poetry. One of only twelve Southern writers invited to the Spoleto Festival USA's forum on the Confederate flag, Ms. Hamilton has been featured on C-SPAN's BookNotes and has made several national radio appearances, including one in 2002 with former NPR anchor Bob Edwards. She is active with the Cave Canem collective, a workshop/retreat for emerging African American poets. And she's a frequent collaborator with artists from the disciplines of performance art, theater, and visual arts—most recently concluding work on "Water Table," a massive installation on the intersections of race, landscape, and culture featured at the 2004 Spoleto Festival USA.

Printed in the United States
71909LV00008B/64-111